PHOTOGRAPHIC MEMORIES
OF THE
LAKE DISTRICT

Front cover picture:
The Pier at Grange Over Sands, 1914

Above:
Stepping Stones at Ambleside, 1888

FRANCIS FRITH & HIS UNIQUE ARCHIVE

In 1860, Francis Frith, the Quaker son of a Chesterfield cooper, was 38 years old. He had already sold a massive grocery business he had built up, for a small fortune. Like Livingstone and Stanley, Frith was fired with a romantic wanderlust, and the Victorian deep passion for travelling and exploring. Between 1857 and '59 he made several pioneering photographic journeys to remote regions of the Nile that brought him considerable fame.

After his marriage in 1860, he confined his wanderings a little closer to home and began a series of photo trips around Britain. His aim was to make his pictures available to the greatest number of people possible - life was hard and drab for millions of Victorians, and Frith believed his 'view souvenirs' of seaside resorts, beauty spots and town and village scenes would help keep their rare days out alive in their memories. He was right: by 1890 he had created the largest photographic publishing company in the world!

As well as thousands of views of high streets around Britain, Frith's growing archive included beautiful scenes of leafy glades, dusty lanes, rocks and coastlines, and the boats and riversides, beloved of Victorian wanderers like Jerome K Jerome - whose 'Three Men in a Boat' had struck a strong chord with the public.

Life in the Frith family was never dull. The family went with him on many trips, and the highlights were recorded by his wife, Mary Ann, in her journal. In 1872 she tells of a relaxing three week expedition to Ilfracombe in North Devon. Whilst such trips may have been something of a holiday for his wife and children, Francis Frith found no time to put his feet up. He was up and down the coast photographing Barnstaple and Lynton, hiring carters to carry him out to remote locations, and boatmen to row him round the bay to view and photograph spectacular cliff formations.

After Francis Frith died in 1898 his sons carried on the business for many years with great success, specialising in postcards and other prints. So impressive is the archive he started that **The Financial Times** called it '*a unique and priceless record of English life in the last century*'.

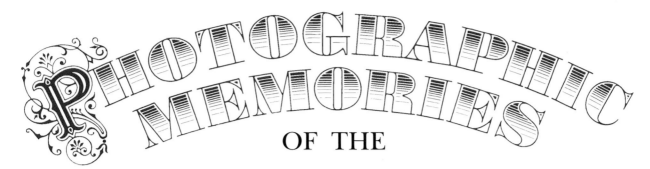

PHOTOGRAPHIC MEMORIES

OF THE

LAKE DISTRICT

THE FRANCIS FRITH COLLECTION

This edition published by
The Francis Frith Collection exclusively for
Selecta Books Ltd., Roundway, Devizes,
Wiltshire SN10 2HR
in association with Michael Brewer.

First published 1995

© The Francis Frith Collection

ISBN 1 85937 015 2

Printed in Singapore

Reproductions of all the photographs in this book
are available as framed or mounted prints. Apply
to The Francis Frith Collection and quote the
title of this book.

The Francis Frith Collection
The Old Rectory, Bimport, Shaftesbury, Dorset SP7 8AT
Tel: 01747 855669 Fax: 01747 855065

Contents

ENDAL. The 'Auld Grey Town' and gateway to the Lakes is set in the lovely valley of the River Kent. Around are majestic vistas of mountain scenery. An old market town, Kendal was famous for its boots, snuff and woollen goods - Flemish weavers settled in the town in medieval times, and Shakespeare talks of three 'knaves' dressed in Kendal green. De Quincey was highly impressed with the townspeople's intellects, saying he encountered *'more natural eloquence'* at Kendal than was to be found *'usually in literary cities or places professedly learned'*.

Right: Nether Bridge, Kendal in 1914. To the south of the town, this graceful old bridge spans the River Kent. Its waters no longer power the mills downstream. They look gentle in the picture but were highly prone to flooding. A stroll along the tree-shaded path by the river has long been a favourite pastime in the town.

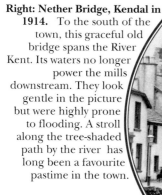

Above: Kendal Market in 1924. The centre of the street is packed solid with traps, carts and motor cars. Traders are selling fruit and vegetables, hardware and dairy produce. On the right is Brunskill's, the classic traditional draper and milliner, offering a bewildering selection of hats, dresses and mantles.

Top: Stramongate Bridge, Kendal in 1924.
The old houses and workshops are clustered on the river bank. In the background.

Left: A distant prospect of Kendal in 1896. The borders of the town are being pushed ever further out. Most of the housing in the foreground is new - built to house the workers in Kendal's thriving industries. Behind the back gardens, just out of the picture, is a huge factory complex with chimney.

Overleaf: Strickland Gate, Kendal, 1888. A vibrant street scene in old Kendal. An elegant lady in white stands in the shadows with a parasol. Her elder daughter pushes the very expensive pram. Her baby is swathed in a cotton turban against the 'harmful' sunlight. The signs show an incredible diversity of businesses all within a few yards: auction rooms, grocer, bed-maker, cheese factor, foundry, brush-maker, monumental sculptor and boot and shoe maker.

Top: Levens Hall near Kendal in 1900. Five miles south of Kendal, the old house at Levens has one of the loveliest gardens in the Lake District, and is celebrated for its magnificent topiary and battlemented hedges. The beech and box are coaxed into strange and wonderful shapes - including chessmen, birds, beasts, a lion and a judge's wig.

Left: Highgate, Kendal, 1914. Children play in one of the town's many old yards that lead off the main streets. Kendal has seen wild times in its history and its streets were built to withstand raids. These yards and passages, now peaceful backwaters with charming stone cottages, were designed to be closed off if an invasion was threatened.

Opposite: Stramongate Yard, Kendal in 1914. With its cobbled floor and plain, harmonious stone cottages, this picturesque yard offers an authentic view of how Kendal must have looked to the Victorians.

Above: Stramongate Bridge, Kendal in 1896.

Left: Collin Croft Yard, Kendal, 1914. Collin Field was one of Kendal's fascinating seventeenth-century houses, owned by the Countess of Pembroke.

Opposite above: Braithwaite Brow, Kendal in 1912. This winding street of small shops looks out to the south of the town. Next to Mr Airey's Refreshment Rooms is the shop of a tripe dresser - a century ago the poor of the town would have flocked to his door when they had a few pence to spare. Buying proper meat from the butcher was a rare treat.

Opposite below: Kendal Castle, 1894. This old motte and bailey dates from the 12th century, and offers fine views of the Lakeland Fells beyond.

WINDERMERE. Ten miles long, and the greatest of England's lakes, Windermere has an incomparable richness of islands, creeks, bays and wooded shores to delight boatman and walker alike. Behind it the mountains rise like a backdrop to a dream. It has its own tiny port - Bowness - where steamers carried trippers out to view the scenery.

Top: The Steam Ferry, Winderemere in 1896. A farmer in his trap and a local carrier enjoy the idyllic chug across the sunlit water. It must be early morning, as there is a lot of space to spare - normally the queue for the crossing would be six deep.

Below: Waterhead, Windermere in 1912. A typically lively scene at the Waterhead pier for trips to Ambleside. Set at the northern tip of the lake, Waterhead is busy and colourful throughout the long summer days, packed with coaches, rowing boats and steamers, conveying trippers to Ambleside or back down the western shore to Lakeside.

Top: Wray Castle, Winderemere, 1886. The boatman poses for the Frith photographer. Did he charge extra for this, or did he welcome the stardom? He would be seen on postcards and prints in every shop in the Lakes. Wray Castle is a modern ruin with tower and battlements. Beatrix Potter and her family used to stay at the house here on family holidays.

Below: The Waterhead Hotel, Windermere in 1887. Hotels sprung up all over Windermere to cope with the huge numbers of tourists who flocked to enjoy its delights. The lake and its surroundings were precisely what the Victorians enjoyed most: wild and majestic scenery that could be reached by coach or steamer, involving not too much exertion.

Overleaf: Windermere in 1887. Boatmen would row visitors out to certain points on the shoreline where they were assured a magnificent vista. Here they stood, the women in their uncomfortable, heavy clothes, taking in the glory of the great outdoors. Then it was back to the hotel for a rest after their exertions and a good dinner.

Top: New villas on the Windermere lakeside, Biskey How, 1887. Wordsworth had raged passionately at the crass insensitivity of new houses and retirement villas built for rich incomers along Windermere and over his beloved hills. You could not travel anywhere at Windermere '*without being offended, at almost every turn, by an introduction of discordant objects, disturbing that peaceful harmony*'. 'The craving for prospect' had caused a rash of new houses '*rising as they do from the summits of naked hills in staring contrast to the snugness and privacy of ancient houses.*' There was much local bitterness.

Left: Rigg's Hotel, Windermere in 1929. Lunch at a prestigious hotel was one of the great delights of a day out in the Lakes.

Opposite: Windermere in about 1870. Here are the Lakes as Wordsworth enjoyed them and battled to keep them - rugged, romantic, unspoiled by man.

Top: The Bowness ferry boat in 1896. A coach and four are carried across the Lake. The horses are steadied by the ferryman, the driver holding the reins in case they bolt: the ferry is steam-driven so a sudden hiss might startle them. The well-to-do passengers sit in silent contemplation of the sublime fells made famous by Wordsworth. **Below: The pleasure steamer 'Teal' at Bowness in 1896.** Things were not always so peaceful. The trippers up from the Lancashire industrial towns could be raucous, laughing, shouting and singing with enjoyment. Worse, there could be 'a nigger troupe' putting on a show on the quay, and a peace-shattering brass band.

Above: Yachts off Bowness in 1896. The Royal Windermere Yacht Club held regular races that were a popular tourist attraction. What more stirring and beautiful prospect could there be than these graceful and silent craft set against the backdrop of the Lakeland mountains?

Left: The Boat Station, Bowness in 1896. It was a long day for trippers. From Blackburn, Burnley and Preston, they have sailed across Morecambe Bay, gone by rail to Lakeside, then by steamer to Ambleside for tea; finally a coach will carry them to Coniston, a train to Barrow, and then a steamer back to Fleetwood and the mills. Who could have begrudged them their day out? The Lakes must have seemed like paradise.

AWKSHEAD. Surrounded by wooded hills and at the head of Esthwaite Water, Hawkshead is 'one of the quaintest of English towns'. Once it was a local centre for cottage weaving, and with its narrow cobbled streets, spacious squares and tangle of arches and passages, it has attracted visitors since Wordsworth's era. Many come to see Ann Tyson's cottage, the house he is supposed to have lived in.

Right: Flag Street, Hawkshead in 1892. Here is a typical Hawkshead street, with overhanging cottages and tall chimneys. The open stream running down the centre of the passage is the Vicarage Beck - there are cloths drying over it. Two years after this photograph was taken this stream was culverted in and is now hidden.

Below: Market Square, Hawkshead in 1930. The creeper-covered cottage is a confectioner's offering Noble's famed 'Hawkshead Cake', a sugary confection of puff pastry filled with currants, spices and candied peel.

Opposite: Garnett's the grocer's, Hawkshead in 1896. Outside the door are two splendid wooden display cases offering Frith & Co's local photographs. Doubtless some of the views on these pages are included.

Above: The lane to the church, Hawskhead in 1892. The postman's trap is filled with sacks of mail and parcels, and is pulled by a donkey. The two men behind him are off for a glass of ale at the Old Inn further down. On the right are the premises of Bryars, builders and wheelwrights.

Left: The Old Pillared Cottage, Hawkshead in 1929. This Hawkshead house - probably built for one of the early wool merchants - has the characteristic stairs up to the first storey. An old lady is weeding her garden plot, which is filled to bursting with achillea.

Opposite top: A Hawkshead square in 1896. The poet A C Gibson described Hawkshead as '*all angles, twists and crooks*'.

Opposite below: Laburnum Street, Hawkshead in 1929. The village offers visitors the unexpected at every turn, with square leading on to square and passages and slated tunnels to delight the eye.

CONISTON. Although much smaller than Windermere, Coniston Water with its beautiful setting has always been a favourite port of call for visitors. The mighty art historian and social critic John Ruskin chose to end his days at Brantwood on its banks. There were copper mines around the village for centuries and rows of miners' cottages. Behind, Coniston Old Man rears its craggy head.

Top: Coniston from the church tower in 1906. The village nestles under the fells. In the centre is the Post Office, with a toddler's pram by the steps. The windows are filled with local photographic views for sale.
Below: Coniston Village in 1929. With its mining days over, Coniston turned its attention to attracting tourists, who drove out from Preston, Blackburn and other industrial towns nearby. A plethora of tearooms has sprung up to meet the challenge.

Above: Coniston, Waterhead in 1912.
Steamers plied up and down the lake
bringing hundreds of day trippers from
Lancashire to enjoy the delights of
Coniston. They set out on the water at
Lakebank at the southern tip. In the
background is what looks like the
luxurious steamboat, Gondola, which
was built in 1859, and was called
*'a perfected combination of the Venetian
gondola and the English steam yacht - having
the elegance, comfort and speed of the latter
and the quiet gliding motion of the former'*.

Left: Tilberthwaite Vale in 1912. This
spectacular valley has all the features of a
Scottish glen. Intrepid Victorian
travellers could climb some rickety steps
to the Ghyll, a romantic gorge where the
'becks run riot'.

AMBLESIDE. Although it has no direct view of Windermere, this thriving market town is set in the park-like valley of the River Rothay, and surrounded by glorious fells. On the main highway through the Lakes, it was once a centre for the sale of cloth, corn, bobbins and bark, and its Whitweek and October fairs were noted for the sale of the local Herdwick sheep.

Right: Ambleside in 1912. With its pavements thronged with people and the continuous rush of traffic - and little left at its heart that could be called historic - Ambleside was very much a place of arrivals and departures, and the perfect spot to be fed and watered. Here visitors await coaches and cars for the return trip home.

Below: The White Lion and Royal Oak Hotels, Ambleside in 1912. People arriving, people leaving, luggage being stowed and unstowed... in 1912, the town has become a large open-air waiting room.

Above: Market Place, Ambleside in 1912. The town in high summer. Carriages almost burst at the seams with passengers. Journeys along the narrow and stony Lakeland roads must have been uncomfortable and often excruciating. Most of the traffic here is still horse-drawn, but there is a 'new fangled' motor car in the distant background. From the Queen's Hotel, coaches left for Keswick and Coniston.

Left: Ambleside from the Gale, 1886. A more peaceful view of the town centre and the Queen's Hotel. The streets are deserted.

Above: Stepping Stones at Ambleside in 1888.

Left: The Bridge House, Ambleside in 1912. Known locally as the applehouse, this unusual little 17th century one-up, one-down house straddles the Stock Beck on the Rydal road. Built as a garden house, with an outside staircase, it is in the care of the National Trust.

Opposite top: Market Square, Ambleside in 1926. Another view of the gable end of the White Lion Hotel. On a signboard by the lamp-post, motor tours taking in eight lakes are being advertised.

Opposite below: Queen's Hotel, Ambleside in 1892. There was always work for a budding porter in this town of hotels. Here a young lad, resplendent in uniform with brass buttons, waits for the next coachload of potential tippers.

Right: Above Troutbeck in about 1870.
A picturesque jumble of gables and
chimneys shows amidst the trees.
Troutbeck offers some of the most
beautiful scenery in Lakeland. Here horses
were watered before the long grind up to
the Kirkstone Pass down to Brothers Water
and Patterdale.

Below: Rydal Water in about 1870. A lady
in a voluminous dark dress sits silently
reading alongside this sublime stretch of
water. Set between Nab Scar and
Loughrigg Fell, its shallows are fringed
with reed in summer. At Rydal,
Wordsworth planted a field with daffodils,
which in spring were a riot of golden
colour.

Above: The summit of Kirkstone Pass in about 1865. An old man with mutton-chop whiskers catches his breath. On the right is the Frith photographer's travelling dark-room, where he laboured in the darkness over trays of fizzing chemicals. On a dark winter's afternoon this rich panaorama of mountains and scree-lined peaks could seem especially bleak, a picture of utter solitude. In summer, however, charabancs , carts and coaches struggled up and down, stopping for refreshments at the 1468 foot high Kirkstone Inn. It was well worth the trip, though. You could then coast gently down the steep incline to Brothers Water, with its rich woodlands and flower-strewn banks.

Left: The Langdale Valley in 1892. A picturesque scene of a humpback bridge with majestic peaks behind.

GRASMERE has been called twice blessed, both for its own natural splendour and beauty, and for the glory brought to it by Wordsworth and the other Lake literary giants, including Coleridge, Southey and De Quincey. Close by the tranquil lake from which it gets its name, it abounds in beautiful scenery - Helm Crag, Rydal Fell, Nab Scar and Silver Howe. It is at the very heart of Lakeland.

Right: Grasmere Vale in 1926. Th road twists between rugged fells from Ambleside through to Keswick. Bubbling streams accompany you at every step.

Above: Red Lion Square, Grasmere in 1926. In the background is the Post Office. Mr Foster the grocer is making the most of the tourists - he has filled his window with china and glass. The walls of the cottages are of coursed local stone, decorative in effect but still hard on the eye when not softened with creeper or rose.

Top: The Rothay Hotel, Grasmere in 1912. Local hotels also organised tours. Here the Rothay Hotel has a prominent signboard over the door announcing that it is a booking office for trips from Ambleside Pier, and for charabancs, omnibuses and coaches. It looks a prestigious establishment: a coach and a carriage are plying for trade and a chauffeur sits waiting patiently.
Below: Wordsworth's Cottage at Grasmere in 1936. On the outskirts of the village, humble Dove Cottage is where Wordsworth wrote some of his finest works. He rented it for £8 a year. This sublime poet loved Grasmere, describing it as '*the loveliest spot that man hath ever found*'.

Right: Grasmere church in 1926.
A contemporary guidebook describes the church as '*a massive but barnlike structure, which no one with an eye to the picturesque would wish to see altered*'. It is one of Lakeland's oldest churches, and Wordsworth is buried in a corner of the churchyard.

Below: Church Stile, Grasmere in 1926. On the left is Hayes' florists and fernery, and on the right the churchyard.

Opposite: Dungeon Ghyll Force in 1888. This is one of the most sublime water-falls in Lakeland. Romantic and majestic, the cliffs rise sheer for a hundred feet, and water plunges into the basin below. Wedged boulders form a natural bridge for walkers, who are helped by two rickety ladders. The Victorians had a special regard for this mysterious, rugged place.

ENRITH. This historic, red, sandstone market town has suffered at the hands of Scottish raiders down the centuries - its castle is now little more than a ruin. It nestles under the wooded slopes of the Beacon. This near 1000 foot high hill carried a flaming beacon as an early warning of impending pillages during the 1745 uprising. Many of the town's outer streets are narrow, making them easier to defend.

Right: Cornmarket, Penrith in about 1950. One of the town's bustling shopping streets, where the old Black Lion coaching inn used to be. Like Kendal, Penrith has a series of yards behind the street buildings which were used as an added defence against Scottish raiders.

Above: King Street, Penrith in about 1950. Note how the Westminster Bank building on the right breaks the general level of the roof lines in the street. From Victorian times, one of the commonest ways banks asserted their local importance was by demolishing old town buildings and erecting 'impressive' new chambers, that more often than not ignored local styles and local building materials. Together with chain stores, they have a lot to answer for in the unfortunate remodelling of many of our old country towns.

Above: Devonshire Street and the Market Place, Penrith in 1893. On market days this broad cobbled space would be thronged with local farmers and animals. Penrith's wide open spaces such as Sandray and Great Dockray were where the townspeople herded their cattle for safety during border raids. Later they became market places.

Left: The Giant's Grave, Penrith churchyard, 1893. This curious thousand year old group of relics - two 11 foot high ruinous crosses and four hogsback tombstones with arched tops and carved like tiles on a roof - were erected to kings or princes in the glorious days when Penrith was the capital of Cumbria. Some say they shelter the remains of the gigantic knight, Owen Caesarius. Sir Walter Scott was fascinated by these artefacts and visited them many times.

Right: Village, Penrith in 1893. A charming picture of children playing and chatting outside St. Andrew's church. With its broad and spacious aisles and squat perpendicular tower, it looks as strong as a fortress.

Below: Eamont Bridge, 1893. This pretty village is a mile out of Penrith on the Shap road. The old trees dapple the cottage walls with shadow, and lean over the street in a way that would never be allowed today, with our regulations about access for high-sided vehicles. On the left is the Crown Hotel.

Top: Mardale, Castle Crag in 1893, and Below: Mardale Church in 1893. This remote village is now only a memory. Once the valley floor was carpeted with wild flowers. Then in the late 1930s, the racing waters of Haweswater were allowed to flood in, destroying the farms, the old inn and the church with its ancient yews, to create a new reservoir for the people of Manchester. Castle Crag, with its prehistoric fortress, still frowns over the sad scene from high above.

Right: the Market Place, Brampton, c 1955.
The old Roman wall is just a mile or two
away. This small brick and sandstone
market town nestles among wooded hills.
In the broad cobbled market square a
Wednesday market has been held since
medieval times. Brampton has one of the
very finest modern churches, with a broad
tower and pencil-thin lead spire. It is
famed for its glorious stained glass by the
Victorian painter Burne-Jones.

Below: Market Place, Brampton, c 1955. In
the background is the 1817 Moot Hall with
its elegant clock tower. Two flights of stairs
lead to an upper room. Alongside this fine
building are the stocks.

Top: Market Cross, Alston in about 1960.
One of Britain's highest market towns, Alston is set in a broad, wooded hollow almost 1000 feet high, its steep cobbled high street climbing up from the banks of the river. Some of the town's old houses have outside staircases leading to the first floor. In the background is the 19th century market cross.

Left: Front Street, Alston in about 1955.
On the right is the Angel Hotel.

Top: Morland in 1893. This picturesque village is set in the valley of the River Lyvennet.

Left: Morland Church in 1893. Many Victorian churches were swathed in ivy. The Victorians were great renovators and restorers, but were also passionate about ruins, which they felt were romantic and sublime. In the case of many villages, though, it could just be the results of a general decline in numbers attending church services. Many fine country churches went almost to rack and ruin a century ago.

Top: Boroughgate, Appleby, about 1955. Tucked away in a wooded valley in a loop of the River Eden, Appleby is one of Lakeland's most historic towns. The town grew up around its Norman castle. For many a long year gypsies have descended on Appleby each year for the famous horse-fair. Here the road up to the castle is shaded with limes. **Below: Market Street, Kirkby Stephen in about 1960.** This charming old market town is set amidst the moors, and has a handsome market hall and some fine historic 17th century houses.

Right: Beck Foot in 1924. This tiny settlement huddles in the valley of the River Lune, overlooked by the lofty Calf, one of a group of steep green hills rising to over 2,000 feet. Traffic on the M6 now thunders by no more than a few yards away.

Below: A picturesque old bridge in Garsdale in 1890. This rugged vale threads its way between Aye Gill Pike and Baugh Fell from Clough to Sedbergh. It must have once been a remote and wild place. Red deer used to come down to feed in the lush valley from the high hills around. Garsdale has many bridges, of which this is one of the oldest. Others, with iron railings, were built after the cloud-burst of 1889. So violent was it, that the waters swelled and flooded, and men ran out to catch the fish that were swept down the lane.

Top: Main Street, Brough in about 1960.
Set on the great road from Carlisle to
York, at the foot of the steep rise over
Stainmore, Brough was an old coaching
town, where the streets and yards echoed
to the clatter of horses' hooves. The
Pennines rise majestically around it. Its
pleasing main street is a mixture of old
stone cottages. On the right is the Castle
Inn.

Left: Brough Village in about 1950. This
view looks the other way - the Castle Inn
is now on the left. Brough has an historic
11th century castle.

SEDBERGH. Lying at the foot of a grassy valley, in the midst of the precipitous Howgill fells, Sedbergh is an ancient market town that grew rapidly in the Victorian era - it was on a strategic turnpike road from Kendal to Kirkby Stephen. In the 1860s the railway came and the town grew even more hectic as the London to Scotland expresses roared by.

Right: Railway Bridge, Sedbergh 1891. A splendid example of Victorian engineering. The railway brought rapid expansion and prosperity to Sedbergh in the mid 1800s.

Below: The market place, Sedbergh in 1894. Solid stone buildings line the town's market area. On the left is a junk shop, offering battered tin trays and buckets and a variety of garden tools such as hoes and rakes. It also sells 'sporting ammunition' and fishing tackle. On the left, just beyond, is a superb Victorian shop front, with arched windows and fancy decorative borders and finials.

Opposite: Sedburgh market in 1923. In the background of this bustling scene is the market hall.

Top: The market place, Sedbergh in 1894. Everyone has taken a welcome break to pose for the Frith cameraman. On the left is a cart selling milk from the churn. The Sedbergh lads stand outside the Post Office. A tough-looking character, possibly a tramp, stands outside the junk shop shown in the picture on the previous page. **Below: The Cricket Ground, Sedbergh in 1901.** In the background, the building with the elegant steeple is Sedbergh's famous school, founded by Roger Lupton in 1525.

Above: Sedbergh from the School House in 1894. Sedbergh is set in majestic surroundings, with high fells and crags all around.

Left: Sedbergh from the hills in 1894. The broad, spacious valley cradles the pleasing little town with its long, straggling main street.

Top: Deepdale, near Dent in 1890. In the shade of mighty Crag Hill, a Victorian artist, sporting a Methuselah-like long white beard, sits among the rocks painting this enchanting waterside scene.

Left: Dent Village from the hay field, 1924. Three hay rakes are propped up in the centre. The haymakers are doubtless chatting to the Frith photographer.

Opposite top: Dent in 1924. It was described in 1902 as consisting of 'two or three twists and curves called streets, cobble-paved from side to side, and a nice inn'. Black marble is a characteristic stone of the village and dale. Two children are drawing water from the village well.

Opposite below: Dent in 1924. On the right is the great megalith boulder of Shap granite bearing the name of the famous geologist, Adam Sedgwick, who was born in the village.

LLSWATER. In the shadow of gaunt Helvellyn, Ullswater offers, in the words of the poet William Wordsworth, '*the happiest combination of beauty and grandeur, which any of the Lakes affords*'. It was along the shores of Ullswater that the poet's sister, Dorothy, first saw the fields of daffodils that '*seemed as if they verily laughed with the wind*'. Wordsworth's poem about this golden 'host' is possibly the most famous poem in the English language.

Right: Ullswater from Place Fell in 1892. The walk up this 2,000 foot mountain was a favourite excursion for the more energetic Victorian traveller. Spectacular vistas across Patterdale into the wooded glens of Grisedale made the stiff climb worthwhile.

Above: Stybarrow Crag, Ullswater in 1888. This romantic and bosky scene below Glencoyne Wood was highly popular with the Victorians, who had a deep passion for the sublime and wild in nature. Here the boatman has rowed the Frith photographer out to record the gnarled rock face and the trees dipping their skirts in the gleaming waters of the lake.

Opposite: Striding Edge, Helvellyn in 1912. Coleridge described a hairaising ascent of this menacing 'dark brow' in 1800: '*No - no! no words can convey any idea of this prodigious wilderness - what a frightfully bulgy precipice I stand on and to my right, how the Crag plunges down, like a waterfall!*'

ESWICK. This peaceful Lakeland town has been a popular holiday centre since Victorian times. Here the River Greta flows through to meet the Derwent, and lofty Skiddaw, awseome and majestic, looks down on the goings-on of the town. Following his great friend and mentor, Wordsworth, Coleridge came to the Lakes, living at Greta Hall with another mighty poet, Southey. Keswick's green vale and mountains have left their mark on English poetry.

Right: Derwent Bridge and Tower Hotel, Keswick in 1889. The River Derwent flows out of Derwentwater into Bassenthwaite. The two lakes were orginally one, but streams flowing towards each other had silted-up and created a new stretch of land between.

Below: A distant view of Keswick in about 1886. Behind, lofty Skiddaw, the 'mountain monarch' of Derwentwater, looms over the town.

Above: The Boat Station at Derwentwater in 1889. Rough and worn stone steps lead out to simple landing stages. A contemporary guidebook said it would not recommend any particular spots to row to. Once embarked, you could not go wrong - the whole lake is beautiful. You could visit the islands or just potter about in the shallows in the deep shadows of the trees.

Left: Ashness Bridge, Keswick in 1893. This old packhorse bridge, on the road to Watendlath, offers visitors a spectacular view of Derwentwater below. The Victorian parties thronged there, their carriages and carts jamming the narrow road. The view downstream is magnificent, with rich woodlands clinging to the flanks of the fells.

Opposite above: Borrowdale and the Borrowdale Hotel in about 1870. Borrowdale has been called the loveliest valley in England. *'Here are smooth fells and rocky crags, wooded slopes and rich pastures, the majesty of mountains seen afar, the music of running water, and the rare magic of Derwentwater that is never twice the same'.* Praise indeed.

Opposite below: The Borrowdale Hotel in 1895. Here, a very formal party, the women swathed in heavy dark dresses and shading themselves from the sun with thick parasols, rests by the hotel porch after an excursion through the valley.

Top: Wastwater in 1889. A tranquil scene of the deepest of the lakes. The view of the rugged scree-covered slopes is breathtaking.

Left: The Victoria Hotel, Wastwater in 1889.

BUTTERMERE. Tucked between Crummock Water and the lake of its own name, Buttermere is set in imposing Lakeland scenery. Yet the tiny village is known for more than its natural splendour: far and wide spread the tragic story of the beautiful and comely Mary, 'Maid of Buttermere'. Mary Robinson, who lived in the Fish Inn (illustrated on the right), was seduced and bigamously married by the Victorian philanderer John Hatfield, who was eventually hanged for forgery. The plight of this poor girl was recounted in copious verses by the Lake Poets.

Right: The Fish Inn, Buttermere, 1919.

Below: An enchanting view of Buttermere in 1889.

Above: The Boat Station at Crummock Water in 1889. Contemporary writers believed Crummock Water to be one of the most beautiful of the Lakes. The hills around were less wild and rugged, and its many inlets and headlands gave it a distinct individuality. At the upper end of the lake is one of the finest waterfalls in England - Scale Force - which has a sheer leap of over 100 feet. The boatman in the picture would doubtless row visitors to see it.

Left: Buttermere in 1889. A stream babbles its way through the village towards the lake. On the right is a back view of the Fish Inn.

COCKERMOUTH. William Wordsworth, Lakeland's most illustrious poet, was born in this old Cumberland market town. It stands where the Cocker and Derwent rivers join their courses - the word 'mot', part of the town's name, means 'meeting of the waters'. Cockermouth boasts a castle, which was built in the 12th century by the Earl of Dunbar.

Right: Cockermouth from the Park, 1906. In the foreground is an impressive municipal drinking fountain, erected in memory of Wordsworth. The sculptured child is his sister Dorothy. Behind it you can just pick out the railway, with a line of goods wagons.

Above: Station Street, Cockermouth in 1906. On the right is the imposing Public Hall, resembling in some ways a giant pin-ball machine with its eccentric tiers and decorative swirls. Further down there is much loading and unloading of wagons and handcarts. A trap is blocking the street completely. **Opposite: Main Street, Cockermouth in 1906.** Men lounge around the slim and elegant clock tower. The fine white statue is of Earl Mayo, the town's M.P. and Viceroy of India.

Right: Cockermouth Castle in 1906. Over the centuries Cumbria has been fought over time and again. The old castle is consequently mostly in ruins.

Below: Wordsworth's house, Cockermouth in 1906. This handsome Georgian house of many windows was where the great poet was born in 1770. It was let free to the family by Sir James Lowther of Lowther Castle. The poet's father was his agent. Here, William, Dorothy and their three brothers lived until 1783. The River Derwent runs along the foot of the garden, so it is no wonder that Wordsworth believed it to be 'the fairest of all rivers'.

Top: King Street, Wigton in about 1955. Described as a *'little workaday town on the fringe of the great fells'*, Wigton is a red sandstone town with a very old market. **Below: Senhouse Street, Maryport in about 1955.** This busy town and port on the Solway Firth has a considerable industrial past, with breweries, tanneries, glass making works, paper mills and coal and iron ore mining. Here is a street of imposing shop fronts, with gilded glass lettering and decorative dentils under the fascia.

ORKINGTON. Set at the mouth of the River Derwent, this busy market town and shipbuilding centre was also a major steel town. Coal was mined from under the sea. The town has a long history: it was called Gabrosentum by the Romans and was the site of one of their forts. When the Lindisfarne monks were fleeing from the Danes, they tried to embark for Ireland from Workington, and their beautifully-illuminated Lindisfarne Gospels fell overboard.

Right: Oxford Street, Workington in about 1955. In the distance on the right is the Oxford cinema. This is one of the town's modern, spacious streets.

Above: Murray Road, Workington in about 1955. On the left is the extravagant Cumberland Bus Station. Victorian terraced houses are hunched between the brash new developments, which show scant respect for the historic nucleus of the town. Similar poor re-development has gone on ever since in towns all over Britain.

Top: Pow Street, Workington in about 1960. Although a relatively recent photograph, the town face it depicts already has a 'period' atmosphere. See the branch of W H Smith on the corner - not a trace of plate glass and plastic in sight. On the right, Marks & Spencer have started the decay - their shop front has completely destroyed the lower half of their building.

Left: The Docks, Workington in about 1950. Around 200 ships were built here in the past hundred years or so.

Right: Main Street, Frizington, about 1950. A small industrial village with a long history of mining. By 1950, with its iron mines closed and much local unemployment, it was showing a sad, grey face.

Below: The Ravenglass and Eskdale Railway in about 1950. This seven mile long narrow-gauge railway was established in 1875 for the transportation of iron and copper ore and stone from the mines and quarries of Eskdale. It joined up with the railway that ran along the coast, carrying the raw materials to Cumbrian industrial plants and factories. It crosses the road from Millom to Whitehaven, climbs Muncaster Fell to Irton, then winds down to Eskdale Green, and on to the terminus beyond Boot. After the decline in mining, it began a new career carrying tourists.

Top: The Square, Cleator Moor in about 1960. This hamlet is set on the edges of the fells in countryside where iron ore has been mined for generations. **Below: Town Hall and Main Street, Egremont in about 1960.** This old iron-mining town is described as 'dull' and 'commonplace' in a turn of the century guidebook. It must have been even duller in later years, after the mining declined and there was much unemployment. Yet all was not gloom: the town's busy Friday market still thrives.

Top: King Street, Egremont in 1912. A bustling street scene in this historic market town. A policeman is directing traffic in the middle of the crossroads as a trolley-bus approaches. On the left you could buy a 1/- ticket for the Winter Gardens.

Below: The Market Place, Egremont in about 1960. Here the street is filled with cars that have already become rare and sought-after classics - the Wolseley, Hillman Minx, sit-up-and-beg Ford Popular and the Renault Dauphine.

Opposite: The Railway Station, Silecroft, c 1955. With Black Fell looming in the background, traffic waits for the Furness coastal train to rumble through the level crossing.

LVERSTON has for many centuries been the market town for the Furness country, set between the green fells and the sea. In the Victorian era it became a centre for ship-building. In addition, the canal, constructed at the end of the previous century to connect the town with the sea, led to Ulverston becoming a strategic local port for the distribution of iron ore, leather, salt and wool.

Right: Market Square, Ulverston in 1921. On the left is Hird's the tea dealer and grocer's, and on the right the fine old shop front of Mason the chemist and druggist.

Below: Market Place, Ulverston in 1912. This marvellous view of an old-style shopping street depicts all the variety and liveliness that we seem to have lost in our town centres today. Here we can see old-established business like Court the Silversmith, a sportsman's outfitter and a confectioner.

Opposite: Lower Market Street, Ulverston in 1921. A bustling street scene with a profusion of trade signs, including the classic 'Lile Bacca Shop'.

Right: The railway at Newby Bridge in 1914. This splendid branch railway ran from Ulverston to Newby Bridge and Lakeside at the foot of Windermere. It was a delightful journey for passengers, the train chugging along the banks of the River Leven, and through rock cuttings and narrow wooded ravines. Haverthwaite, the village shown in the previous photograph, was on the line.

Below: Haverthwaite Village. A charming old-world cobbled alley in a picturesque village a few mile south of Lakeside, Windermere. Note the cottage pump on the left.

Top: Newby Bridge in 1914. This narrow and historic hump-backed bridge crosses the Leven below Windemere. In the background is the Swan Hotel, where trippers bound for Windermere caught coaches to Lakeside. Children play on the banks. The family has hired a rowing boat for the afternoon. The reflections in the water create a harmonious and peaceful scene. On the right and in the foreground of the picture are what are probably the cast-offs of a local boat builder.

Left: The Leven at Newby Bridge in 1914. Lush woods stretch alongside the banks of the river, making a boat the best way to enjoy its lower reaches and the southern tip of Windermere.

ARK is a pleasing jumble of cottages, farms and inns, set around a series of streams and bridges. Set on the Cartmel peninsula, it has a long tradition of fishing, especially for cockles and mussels, on the vast expanses of sands on the estuary of the River Leven. It was also a mill town. Moreover, it had grand connections: nearby is Holker Hall, begun in 1580, and the home of the Cavendish family.

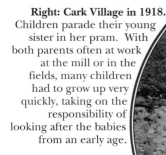

Right: Cark Village in 1918. Children parade their young sister in her pram. With both parents often at work at the mill or in the fields, many children had to grow up very quickly, taking on the responsibility of looking after the babies from an early age.

Above: Lower Row, Cark in 1897. This lovely old row of terraced cottages with their whitewashed window and door rebates and informal front gardens, leads to the mill beyond. It looms over the village with its tall chimney. A stream gurgles along at the side of the lane.

Above: Cark House, Cark in 1897. The stream bubbles below this handsome hump-backed bridge, which casts mesmerising reflections in the water.

Left: The Entrance to the Mill, Cark in 1897. This attractive entrance house, with its chunky stone dressings and rusticated archway, leads to the substantial mill building that can be seen in the photograph on the previous page.

CARTMEL. This most attractive of towns is set amongst woods and gentle rolling hills, and is renowned for its Priory Church. According to ancient legend, monks came to Cartmel and began to build a priory on the hill. But a voice commanded them to build it in a valley between two streams, one flowing north, the other south. They searched far and wide in vain for months, then returned disconsolate to Cartmel, only to find that its streams fulfilled the condition precisely. Thus the town began.

Right: Market Place and Cross, Cartmel in 1894. In the background is the historic Abbey Gateway. Note Mr Overend's tiny one-up one-down draper's shop to the right.

Below: Devonshire Place, Cartmel in 1912. This marvellous photograph, with the beautiful Priory Church in the background, offers insights into the news stories of the day. '*Grave Textile Decisions*' in the Leeds Mercury, '*Chief Scout writes about the Jamboree*' in the Mail, '*Navy Cuts - Admiralty Order*' in the Daily News, and '*Champion Jockey Injured*' in the Daily Despatch.

Opposite: A peep through the Abbey Gateway in 1912. On the left, near the end, is Ayers' Old Fashioned Eating House.

RANGE-OVER-SANDS. Backed by wooded hills, and in a sheltered position, this one-time fishing village grew rapidly into a thriving resort town in Victorian times. With its vistas of the broad sweep of Morecambe Bay, and with a mile of breezy promenade, a small pier and jetty for boats, 'the Torquay of the North' has long been a favourite holiday town with Lancastrians.

Right: The Promenade, Grange-over-Sands in 1914. The mile-long Promenade is shown here at its eastern end. Grange is blessed with a mild climate, and the public gardens are filled with rare and exotic trees and shrubs.

Above: Main Street, Grange-over-Sands in 1906. Note the delightful series of matching shop fronts on the right, with ornate carved fascia boards and turned finials. Although it was called the 'Torquay of the North', Grange was much smaller than its Devon counterpart, and was for those who preferred the quiet life. There was nothing brash about Grange. Its main street, shown here, could hardly be compared with the grand commercial thoroughfares of Torquay.

Above: The Promenade and Pierhead, Grange-over-Sands in 1921. A man sits with a stack of deckchairs waiting for customers. The tide has only just begun to go out and the beach is still quiet.In the distance are the softly-rounded wooded hills that give the town such a uniquely attractive situation.

Left: A Grange-over-Sands street scene in 1894. On the left is the Working Men's Institute.

Overleaf: Disembarking from the sail boats, 1914. In the distance, people are walking in all directions across the wide sweep of sands.

Top: Grange-over-Sands in 1906. A view of the town from the beach. The tide is out and in the centre of the photograph is the pierhead.

Left: Grange-over-Sands in 1912. A welcome rest for a hardworking boatman.

Opposite above: The Beach, Grange-over-Sands, in 1896. The town sits gently on the flanks of the wooded hills. When the tide was out you could walk for miles.

Opposite below: A round of tennis, Grange-over-Sands in 1894. Since the ladies are playing in full length dresses, the game they played was inevitably more sedate than the modern equivalent.

Opposite above: The market square, Milnthorpe in about 1950. This ancient and delightful market town was formerly the country's seaport. It has a well preserved cross with a particularly chilling feature. At its foot, welded into the steps of the base, are iron ankle cuffs.

Opposite below: The cross roads, Milnthorpe in about 1950.

Top: Barbon Village in 1901. The Barbon Beck tumbles its way down from the Pennines to join the River Lune, splashing through this pleasing old stone village under a packhorse bridge.

Left: Devil's Bridge, near Kirkby Lonsdale in 1899. This ancient bridge, with its wide graceful arch probably dates from the 13th century.

KIRKBY LONSDALE. John Ruskin praised this old market town fulsomely, saying it had moorland, sweet river, and English forest at their best. Markets have been held here since medieval times. In the past it was an important coaching stop on the great roads to the North, but its visitors now are predominately tourists to the lovely valley of the River Lune.

Previous page: Kirkby Lonsdale in 1899. Market day in the town. The first traders, their wares stored in rush baskets, are about to set up their stalls.

Right: Main Street, Kirkby Lonsdale in 1908. On the left is the Red Dragon and further down the street, the Green Dragon.

Above: The Main Street, Kirkby Lonsdale in about 1899. On the left is the Royal Hotel, with its ornate wrought iron verandah above the porch, and Cyclists Touring Club signboard. The town's old squares and elegant Georgian buildings give it a timeless charm. In the background is the narrow main street, packed with small shops and businesses.

Top: Kirkby Lonsdale in 1908. Children pose under the old jettied stone house on the left. In the background is an old-style butcher's shop. **Above: The market square, Kirkby Lonsdale in 1908.** This picture shows the new market cross, considered an ugly addition to the square. The remains of the old cross were to be found opposite the Abbot's Hall.

Index